The Best Popsicle Recipes for Kids and Adults

Simple Popsicle Cookbook for The Tastiest Icy Treats

BY: Valeria Ray

License Notes

A Special Reward for Purchasing My Book!

Thank you, cherished reader, for purchasing my book and taking the time to read it. As a special reward for your decision, I would like to offer a gift of free and discounted books directly to your inbox. All you need to do is fill in the box below with your email address and name to start getting amazing offers in the comfort of your own home. You will never miss an offer because a reminder will be sent to you. Never miss a deal and get great deals without having to leave the house! Subscribe now and start saving!

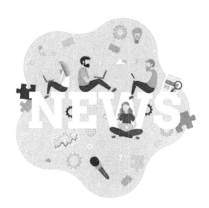

SUBSCRIBE
——TO NEWSLETTER——

https://valeria-ray.gr8.com

Contents

Homemade Popsicle Recipes...................................... 6

(1) Rainbow Popsicles.. 7

(2) Fruit Salad Popsicles..................................... 11

(3) Very Green Popsicles..................................... 14

(4) Simple Banana Shakes Popsicles 17

(5) Banana and Chocolate Popsicles................... 20

(6) Cereal Popsicles 23

(7) Virgin Pina Colada Popsicles....................... 26

(8) Matcha Green and Chocolate Popsicles 29

(9) Strawberries Yogurt Popsicles...................... 32

(10) Lemonade Popsicles................................... 35

(11) Thai Tea Popsicles..................................... 38

(12) Vanilla and Coconut Popsicle 41

(13) Sugar Free Cherry Popsicles 44

(14) Lime Popsicle.. 46

(15) Mojito Popsicles 49

(16) Spicy Mango Popsicles 52

(17) Dark Chocolate Popsicles... 55

(18) Blueberries Popsicles 58

(19) Peaches and Ginger Popsicles..................................... 61

(20) Bone Broth Popsicles 64

(21) Watermelon Popsicles 67

(22) Frozen Bananas with Multiple Toppings..................... 70

(23) Maple Syrup and Coffee Popsicles 73

(24) Orange and Pineapple Popsicles................................. 75

(25) Berries Popsicles in A Bowl 78

About the Author... 81

Author's Afterthoughts.. 83

Homemade Popsicle Recipes

MMMMMMMMMMMMMMMMMMMMMMMMMMMMMMM

(1) Rainbow Popsicles

We will use fresh fruits to prepare these popsicles but will layers the colors and flavors. It will be beautiful, colorful, tasty and fun to make, what could we ask for me for this very last recipe of this great cookbook?

List of Ingredients:

- 1 large ripped mango
- 3 medium kiwis
- 1 cup fresh raspberries
- 1 cup fresh blackberry
- 4 cups water
- 4 tablespoons Raw honey

Makes: 4-6

Total Prep Time: 60 minutes + before you can eat them!

MMMMMMMMMMMMMMMMMMMMMMMMMMMMM

Preparation:

This is how you will go about making these lovely popsicles.

You will blend and freeze the popsicles step by step, or fruit by fruit.

Use the fruit with one cup of water and 1 tablespoon of raw honey.

I like to start with the blackberries. So, I will blend until the texture is smooth. I will fill the popsicles molds a little less than a ¼ full. Freeze for an hour or so.

Next, I will blend the mango with water and honey together.

Add on top of the blackberries in the molds and freeze again.

Next, I will add the kiwis with water and honey in the blender. Blend until smooth and add into to the popsicles molds. Freeze again for a little while, before adding the last fruit layer.

Place the raspberries, water and honey in the blender. Activate and then add to the popsicles.

Freeze again for another hour or so.

Once you get the popsicles out next time, they will have 4 different levels of colors.

You could add more levels, more fruits.

(2) Fruit Salad Popsicles

These popsicles will make you wish you could eat fruits presented to you like this every day of the week. I think it is a great way to interest your kids into discovering perhaps new fruits or adding their favorites in there if they already are good fruits eater. Visit your farmer's market or local produce stand and pick a few different fruits and start preparing these beautiful frozen treats.

List of Ingredients:

- 3 sliced kiwis
- 2 cups fresh sliced strawberries
- 1 cup blueberries
- 1 1/2 cup orange juice
- 1 1/2 cup coconut milk
- 3 tablespoons agave syrup

Makes: 4-6

Total Prep Time: 60 minutes + before you can eat them!

MMMMMMMMMMMMMMMMMMMMMMMMMMMMMM

Preparation:

The trick with this recipe is to try to make it look like a fruit salad on a stick!

In the blender, you will only mix the agave syrup, coconut milk and orange juice.

You will wash and prepare the fresh fruits.

Pour the popsicle mixture half way into the molds.

Add a little of each fruit into each popsicle mold.

Freeze and enjoy seeing the beautiful colors and whole fruits on a stick!

(3) Very Green Popsicles

I do make green smoothies quite regularly. So, the other day, I thought to myself, why not making some popsicles out of that smoothie mixture! And I did. I was even able to convince my kids to try them.

List of Ingredients:

- 1 small seedless cucumber
- 1 cup baby spinach leaves
- 2 chopped celery stalks
- 2 smalls sliced Granny smith apples
- 3 cups soy milk
- 1 tablespoon minced fresh ginger
- 2 tablespoons agave syrup

Makes: 4-6

Total Prep Time: 60 minutes + before you can eat them!

MMMMMMMMMMMMMMMMMMMMMMMMMMMMMM

Preparation:

Prepare the fruits and veggies as instructed.

Add half of all the ingredients in the blender at first.

Activate until the mixture is smooth.

Pour into half of the popsicle molds.

Repeat the same action for the second half of the ingredients and when done pour the mixture into the remaining molds.

Freeze for a few hours before you can enjoy these very green treats.

(4) Simple Banana Shakes Popsicles

We have made a popsicle containing banana slices, now let's make one that contains banana mousse. My mother used to always make banana mousse, with egg whites. It was so fluffy and delicious, we could not wait until some over-ripe bananas would become available again. She never considered making popsicles out of them, but I can't blame her, we probably always were devouring that dessert quick!

List of Ingredients:

- 3 large ripe bananas
- 2 cups soy milk
- 1 teaspoon vanilla extract
- 2 tablespoons chia seeds
- 1 teaspoon lemon juice

Makes: 4-6

Total Prep Time: 60 minutes + before you can eat them!

MMMMMMMMMMMMMMMMMMMMMMMMMMMMMMM

Preparation:

In a mixing bowl, mash the bananas with a fork.

Add the lemon juice, vanilla extract and ½ cup of milk.

Use an electric mixer to bring it to a mousse and set aside.

Place the rest of the milk in the high-speed blender container and add the chia seeds.

Let them sit for about 5 minutes.

Add the bananas mousse and activate for a minute or so.

Pour this mixture into the popsicles molds and freeze.

It should be ready several hours later.

(5) Banana and Chocolate Popsicles

This popsicle recipe will combine chocolate and bananas. It is already a very delicious and popular combination. But, don't be fooled, we will not mash the bananas, but only slice them. So, on top of being delicious, it will be very fun to look at and to eat of course!

List of Ingredients:

- 2 cups cashew milk
- 2 tablespoons cashew butter
- 1/3 cup favorite chocolate syrup
- 2 sliced bananas
- 1 cup semi-sweet chocolate chips
- ½ cup chopped walnuts
- 2 tablespoons coconut oil

Makes: 4-6

Total Prep Time: 60 minutes + before you can eat them!

MMMMMMMMMMMMMMMMMMMMMMMMMMMMM

Preparation:

In your high-speed blender, combine the chocolate syrup, cashew milk and cashew butter.

Place the mixture in the popsicles molds and add some sliced banana in each of them.

Freeze the popsicles for a few hours.

Meanwhile, melt the chocolate chips and coconut oil in the microwave.

Let the chocolate cool down.

In a separate bowl, place the coconut.

Get your popsicles out of the freeze, and for the one you are ready to eat, dip in the chocolate mixture and then in the coconut.

Enjoy right away!

(6) Cereal Popsicles

Nothing is easier than making your kid eat breakfast when it's about their favorite cereals. It will be the same with these popsicles. You can do it with healthy cereals and get them use to eat less sugary treats if that's your goal.

List of Ingredients:

- 1 cup dry favorite cereals
- 2 cups whole milk
- 2 tablespoons cacao powder
- 1 tablespoon maple syrup (if the cereals are not very sweet already)
- 1 cup Greek yogurt

Makes: 4-6

Total Prep Time: 60 minutes + before you can eat them!

MMMMMMMMMMMMMMMMMMMMMMMMMMMMMM

Preparation:

Combine the cacao powder to the yogurt and set aside for now.

In the blender, add the milk with the maple syrup and chocolate yogurt

Blend until smooth for a minute or so.

Now get ready to add the cereals and milk mixture to the popsicles molds.

Make sure you do make the popsicles molds overflow.

So, add ¼ mold in cereals and fill up the rest with milk mixture.

Freeze the popsicles for a few hours and enjoy for breakfast or as treats!

(7) Virgin Pina Colada Popsicles

Pina Colada sounds so refreshing and evokes the taste of summer, it's perfect pineapple and coconut flavor is a must to make during the hotter months of the year. Of course, if you are serving the popsicles to children, you will need to keep them alcohol free. We will show you how. It's all about coconut and pineapple!

List of Ingredients:

- 2 cans coconut milk with cream
- 1 cup fresh chopped pineapple or canned if you can't use fresh
- 1 teaspoon agave syrup
- 1 teaspoon vanilla extract
- 1 cup coconut water
- 1/4 cup agave nectar

Makes: 4-6

Total Prep Time: 60 minutes + before you can eat them!

MMMMMMMMMMMMMMMMMMMMMMMMMMMMMM

Preparation:

Prepare you fresh pineapple and cut it in small pieces. If you are using canned pineapple, I suggest you use the diced ones.

In the high-speed blender container place the coconut water, vanilla extract, agave syrup and pineapple.

Activate until you are satisfied with the result. If you like some pineapple chunks in your popsicles, don't overdo it.

Add the coconut milk and mix again for 30 seconds.

Pour the mixture int the popsicles molds.

Freeze for a few hours before you can have one!

(8) Matcha Green and Chocolate Popsicles

Making matcha green popsicles seems like the next logical thing to do since it is a popular superfood as well. I like to add a touch of chocolate, for a little extra taste, but also for the appearances. It is so beautiful to combine that dark brown on the bright green.

List of Ingredients:

- 2 Tablespoons matcha green powder
- 1 ripped banana
- 2 cups rice milk
- 2 Tablespoons lime juice
- 1 tablespoon lime zest
- 1 tablespoon agave syrup

Chocolate sauce

- ¼ cup heavy cream
- 3 Tablespoons sweet butter
- 4 Tablespoons Cacao powder
- 1 tablespoon agave syrup

Makes: 4-6

Total Prep Time: 60 minutes + before you can eat them!

MMMMMMMMMMMMMMMMMMMMMMMMMMMMMM

Preparation:

In the high-speed blender, place the matcha green, lime zest, lime juice, agave syrup, banana and half of the milk.

Activate until the mixture is smooth, add the rest of the milk and blend again.

Pour that mixture into the popsicles molds and freeze.

Meanwhile, place all the ingredients for the chocolate sauce in a medium saucepan.

Stir and keep on medium heat until the mixture is totally smooth.

Remove from the heat and let it cool down completely.

When you get a popsicle out, dip it into the chocolate sauce, before enjoying it fully.

(9) Strawberries Yogurt Popsicles

I love strawberries and to be able to make my children popsicles containing fresh strawberries is just amazing. It's going back to the sources. Our ancestors did not have the luxury to purchase some pre-made popsicles, cakes, cookies and other treats. So, let's go pick our berries, or at least buy them from a fresh produce market and start making these delicious popsicles.

List of Ingredients:

- 1 cup whole milk
- 2 cups fresh sliced strawberries
- 1 teaspoon vanilla extract
- 2 tablespoons white sugar
- 1 tablespoon lemon juice
- 1 cup water

Makes: 4-6

Total Prep Time: 60 minutes + before you can eat them!

MMMMMMMMMMMMMMMMMMMMMMMMMMMM

Preparation:

In the blender, combine the fresh strawberries, white sugar, vanilla extract, water and lemon juice.

Activate for a few minutes and then add the milk.

Activate again.

If you prefer some of the fruits to be intact, you can add the strawberries towards the end and avoid blending completely.

Pour the mixture into the popsicles molds.

Freeze for a few hours before you can enjoy!

(10) Lemonade Popsicles

Drinking a lemonade is really refreshing. So, eating a popsicle made from lemonade is no different. Now, I am talking about homemade lemonade here of course, where you squeeze the lemons and all. Let's get started.

List of Ingredients:

- 4 cups water
- 2 cups fresh squeeze lemon juice
- 3 tablespoons lemon zest
- ¼ cup agave syrup
- 6 minced mint leaves

Makes: 4-6

Total Prep Time: 60 minutes + before you can eat them!

MMMMMMMMMMMMMMMMMMMMMMMMMMMMMM

Preparation:

In a large pitcher, combine the water, lemon juice and lemon zest. Add the agave syrup and stir.

Also add the mint leaves and stir again.

Refrigerate so all ingredients marry well together.

After an hour or so, place in the blender and activate until all is well blended.

Pour the mixture into the popsicles molds and freeze for a few hours.

You will enjoy these frozen treats on a hot summer day.

(11) Thai Tea Popsicles

If you like drinking tea, you will like this frozen treat as well. You could really use the type of tea you prefer, green tea, earl grey tea or others. I suggest the Thai tea because it is slightly spicy and very tasty, so it will certainly be a unique popsicle to make. I love to add lemon or lime juice, but some neighbors of mine have tried it with orange juice and they love it as well.

List of Ingredients:

- 4 bags Thai tea
- 4 cups water
- 1 teaspoon vanilla extract
- 2 minced mint leaves
- 2 cups coconut milk
- 1 can sweet condensed milk
- Pinch cinnamon

Makes: 4-6

Total Prep Time: 60 minutes + before you can eat them!

MMMMMMMMMMMMMMMMMMMMMMMMMMMMMM

Preparation:

Boil water in a medium saucepan.

Add the Thai tea bags and let them infuse for at least 10 minutes.

Remove the tea bags and let the tea cool down a little.

In the blender, add the condensed milk, mint leaves, cinnamon, vanilla extract and tea.

Activate for a few minutes.

Finally add the coconut milk and activate again.

Pour this lovely mixture into the popsicles molds.

Freeze a few hours.

Enjoy on a hot summer day.

(12) Vanilla and Coconut Popsicle

We are going coconut all the way! We will use coconut water, coconut milk and shredded coconut. So, if you are not crazy about coconut, this is not the right frozen dessert for you. Don't forget that you are free to also add other ingredients such as nuts (pistachios marry well).

List of Ingredients:

- 2 cups coconut milk
- 1 cup coconut cream
- 1 cup coconut flakes
- ½ teaspoons vanilla extract
- 2 tablespoons agave syrup
- ½ cup pistachios (no shell)

Makes: 4-6

Total Prep Time: 60 minutes + before you can eat them!

MMMMMMMMMMMMMMMMMMMMMMMMMMMMMM

Preparation:

In the food processor, place the coconut flakes and the pistachios.

Activate until it is reduced in powder.

Add the powder you created with the coconut milk and cream in the blender.

Also add next the agave syrup and the vanilla in the blender.

Activate and blend until this mixture is beautiful smooth.

Pour into the popsicle molds.

Freeze until form.

(13) Sugar Free Cherry Popsicles

These frozen treats might look and taste a lot like the popsicles you can buy at the grocery store. However, you will be able to make them for much cheaper and you will know exactly what they contain. My girlfriends love when I make these because they don't have to cheat on their diet.

List of Ingredients:

- 3 cups water
- 3 cups fresh sliced strawberries
- ¾ cup stevia

Makes: 4-6

Total Prep Time: 60 minutes + before you can eat them!

MMMMMMMMMMMMMMMMMMMMMMMMMMMMMMM

Preparation:

In a medium saucepan, place all the ingredients.

Bring to boil and stir. Continue cooking on low temperature for about 20 minutes or until fruits seem to be fully cooked.

Let that mixture cook down.

Place it in the blender next.

Activate for several minutes or until mixture is total smooth

Pour into the popsicles molds.

Freeze until firm.

(14) Lime Popsicle

These popsicles will make you happy. Just like eating a piece of key lime pie makes you happy. You can skip the pie crust, so less carbs. You can also skip the whipped cream, so again less calories and less carbs. I love making the treats with coconut milk, I can also skip there some calories and enjoy 2 popsicles instead of one!

List of Ingredients:

- 1 large ripped avocado sliced
- ½ cup lime juice
- 2 tablespoons lime zest
- 2 cans coconut milk with cream
- 1 cup Greek yogurt
- 3 Tablespoons stevia

Makes: 4-6

Total Prep Time: 60 minutes + before you can eat them!

MMMMMMMMMMMMMMMMMMMMMMMMMMMMMM

Preparation:

Peel and pit the avocado. Cut it into slices and place it in the blender.

Add the lime juice, lime zest and coconut milk, along with the stevia.

Activate until smooth.

Add the yogurt and blend again for another minute.

Pour the mixture into the popsicles molds and freeze away.

This will be as close as key lime pie as you get on a stick!

(15) Mojito Popsicles

These popsicles are for adults only. Why? Simply because they do contain alcohol. So, a traditional mojito is made with white rum, fresh mint leaves, lime juice, sugar and soda water. We are tweaking the original version a little, but you will still recognize the lime and run. If you have children, make sure you replace the rum with lemonade or perhaps green tea, so everyone can enjoy one.

List of Ingredients:

- 2 cups lime juice
- 2 cups water
- 2 tablespoons lime zest
- 4 ounces white rum
- 4-6 minced mint leaves
- 4 tablespoons white sugar
- 1 cup Sprite or any lime-flavored soda

Makes: 4-6

Total Prep Time: 60 minutes + before you can eat them!

MMMMMMMMMMMMMMMMMMMMMMMMMMMMMMMM

Preparation:

Place the lime juice, lime zest, mint leaves, white sugar and water in the blender.

Activate until all is well blended.

Place in a pitcher and add the tum and the soda.

Stir well.

Pour into the popsicles molds.

You should plan to let them freeze for at least 4 hours before removing from the molds.

Keep them away from kids!

(16) Spicy Mango Popsicles

When I say very spicy, I really mean it is going to make your mouth "feel like it's on fire". However, you can certainly choose a different spice than cayenne pepper and keep it more accessible. Turmeric, nutmeg and cinnamon are also all good choice when you use mango as your main ingredient. It is all about preferences and whom you are serving these popsicles too.

List of Ingredients:

- 3 cups cubed fresh mango
- ½ cup pineapple juice
- 2 cups coconut milk
- ½ teaspoons cayenne pepper
- Pinch cinnamon

Makes: 4-6

Total Prep Time: 60 minutes + before you can eat them!

MMMMMMMMMMMMMMMMMMMMMMMMMMMMMM

Preparation:

Get your fresh mango out and peel them

Cut them into pieces or cubes and place the fruit in the blender.

Add the pineapple juice, cayenne pepper and cinnamon, and 1 cup of coconut milk.

Activate for a few minutes.

Add the rest of the coconut milk and activate again.

Pour the mixture into the popsicles molds.

Freeze for a few hours and get ready to be surprised by this spicy treat!

(17) Dark Chocolate Popsicles

Have you heard that dark chocolate can be good for you? You were praying it was right and your prayers have been answered. In moderation, dark chocolate can certainly be good for you as it contains antioxidants. Let's put it that way, if you are going to choose a type of chocolate to have, dark chocolate is a very good option. So, let's make dark chocolate popsicles for all these moms who want to treat themselves and feel completely guilt free.

List of Ingredients:

- 1 cup water
- 2 Tablespoons dark cacao powder
- 1/3 cup coconut palm sugar
- 2 cups whole milk
- ½ teaspoons almond extract

Makes: 4-6

Total Prep Time: 60 minutes + before you can eat them!

MMMMMMMMMMMMMMMMMMMMMMMMMMMMM

Preparation:

In a saucepan, combine the water, dark chocolate and palm sugar.

Heat on medium temperature and stir until the mixture is free of lumps.

Let it cool down a little.

Add to the blend container and add the milk and almond extract also.

Activate for several minutes.

Pour the chocolate mixture into the popsicles molds.

Freeze for at least a few hours before you can enjoy!

(18) Blueberries Popsicles

You could use yogurt, milk or even half and half for this recipe. However, I am going all the way and using some heavy cream. It is a special treat when I make these, and obviously if you have health issues requiring you to lower the fat your intake, use a substitute as previously mentioned. Of course, fresh blueberries are a requirement.

List of Ingredients:

- 1 cup heavy cream
- 1 cup coconut milk
- 2 cups fresh blueberries
- 2 tablespoons raw honey
- ½ teaspoons vanilla extract

Directions:

Makes: 4-6

Total Prep Time: 60 minutes + before you can eat them!

MMMMMMMMMMMMMMMMMMMMMMMMMMMMMM

Preparation:

Simply dump the blueberries and coconut milk in the high speed blender container.

Activate until the blueberries are totally smooth.

Add the heavy cream, raw honey and vanilla next and activate again.

Pour this very creamy and sweet mixture into the popsicles molds.

Freeze until form and enjoy!

(19) Peaches and Ginger Popsicles

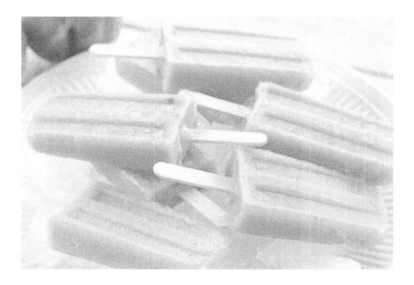

Again, freshness is the key. So, get those fresh peaches form the market and get ready to reap some awesome popsicles for everyone. I like to use yogurt with the peaches, it makes it very tasty and the consistence is perfect as well. I purposely leave some chunks of peaches, so it tastes even more naturally with each bite.

List of Ingredients:

- 4 medium peaches peeled and sliced
- 1 cup pineapple juice
- 1 cup orange juice
- 1 cup coconut water
- ½ cup plain yogurt
- 2 Tablespoons maple syrup
- Pinch ground ginger
- Pinch ground cinnamon

Makes: 4-6

Total Prep Time: 60 minutes + before you can eat them!

MMMMMMMMMMMMMMMMMMMMMMMMMMMMM

Preparation:

Wash, peel and slice the fresh peaches.

In the high speed blender container, add the peaches, pineapple juice and orange juices.

Blend for a few minutes.

Add the spices, maple syrup coconut water and yogurt.

Activate again and blend until you are satisfied with the consistency.

If you like a few pieces of peach, do not overdo it.

Pour the final mixture in the popsicles molds and freeze.

After a few hours, you can finally taste!

(20) Bone Broth Popsicles

We all know how bone broth has been advertised as being so beneficial for your health lately. That is true. I never thought I would think about making popsicle out if it, but it occurred to me that many times during the summer season, I don't feel like eating a hot broth. I do however want to continue to benefit from the wonderful properties they offer. So, an idea was born!

List of Ingredients:

- 4 cups bone broth
- 1 cup water
- Recipe for chicken bone broth
- 2-pounds of any of these parts: chicken necks/feet/wings
- 2 large sliced carrots
- 2 chopped celery stalks
- 1 medium chopped onion
- 2 Tablespoons minced garlic
- 1/3 cup fresh minced parsley with oregano and thyme
- 2 bay leaves
- 12-14 cups water
- Salt, black pepper

Makes: 4-6

Total Prep Time: 60 minutes + before you can eat them!

MMMMMMMMMMMMMMMMMMMMMMMMMMMMMM

Preparation:

Before you can make bone broth popsicles, you must prepare the bone broth.

You should plan to prepare the broth the day before.

In a large saucepan, simply combine all ingredients listed under the bone broth.

Bring to boil and then reduce the temperature and let it cook for a few hours.

You will then use a strainer, once the broth has cooled down, to sort the broth form the larger pieces.

You should be left only with the liquid part.

Make sure you remove the bay leaves also.

To make the popsicles, you will add water to the bone broth and stir well.

You will then fill the popsicles mold and freeze them for a few hours at least.

This is not a sweet treat, but it is a health one!

(21) Watermelon Popsicles

Watermelon is a very refreshing fruit. To make popsicles out of it seems logical. It is a very good fruit to eat when you are following low calorie diet or low carb diet. Now, to kick it up a notch, we will mix in another type of fruit with it. Can you guess?

List of Ingredients:

- 4 cups fresh watermelon (cubed or diced)
- ¼ cup. lemon juice
- 1 tablespoon lemon zest
- 1 cup water
- 3 tablespoons white sugar

Makes: 4-6

Total Prep Time: 60 minutes + before you can eat them!

MMMMMMMMMMMMMMMMMMMMMMMMMMMMMM

Preparation:

Cut the watermelon into cubes or buy it already cubed.

Place half of the fruits in the high-speed blender container with the lemon juice and lemon zest and the sugar.

Activate for a few minutes.

Add the rest of the watermelon and the water (if you judge necessary).

Activate until consistency is perfect.

Pour into the popsicles mold and freeze.

Get ready for a refreshing treat a few hours later.

(22) Frozen Bananas with Multiple Toppings

These frozen treats are made from entire bananas. You will be surprised how easy they are to make and how fast your kids will eat them. I often make these when I have a pool party and a mixture of adults and kids, as both end up loving these frozen bananas with some yummy toppings.

List of Ingredients:

- 3 bananas cut in half
- ½ cup chopped roasted peanuts
- 1/3 cup shredded sweetened coconut
- 1 cup plain Greek yogurt
- Handful of chocolate sprinkles

Makes: 4-6

Total Prep Time: 60 minutes + before you can eat them!

MMMMMMMMMMMMMMMMMMMMMMMMMMMMM

Preparation:

Peel and cut the bananas in half.

Make sure you use some firm bananas, as you have to insert a popsicle stick in each one.

In a mixing bowl, combine the chocolate sprinkles, peanuts and coconut.

Dip each banana half way in the toppings mixture you made and lay them on parchment paper on a plate freeze friendly.

Freeze for about two hours and get ready to taste some amazing frozen bananas.

(23) Maple Syrup and Coffee Popsicles

I am a coffee lover, big time. So, any desserts made with coffee, I usually love. This popsicle is my signature recipe, and only for me and my husband to enjoy, as our kids, think coffee has a bitter taste. I like to add maple syrup as a natural sweetener so they can enjoy them as well.

List of Ingredients:

- 2 cups water
- 2 tablespoons instant coffee
- 4 Tablespoons maple syrup
- 2 cups cashew milk
- 1 tablespoon flaxseeds

Makes: 4-6

Total Prep Time: 60 minutes + before you can eat them!

MMMMMMMMMMMMMMMMMMMMMMMMMMMMMMMM

Preparation:

Bring to boil the water and add the instant coffee.

Let it sit and col down for 10 minutes.

In the high-speed blender, add the flaxseeds, cashew milk, maple syrup and coffee.

Blend until the mixture is totally acceptable for popsicles.

Pour into the molds and freeze for a few hours before you can lick away!

(24) Orange and Pineapple Popsicles

Orange and pineapple popsicles are possibly the most divine frozen treat. The freshness of the fruits, the sunniness of the color and the happy feeling you get when you eat one, nothing can go wrong. Use some fresh ingredients, and all will be well.

List of Ingredients:

- 2cups fresh chopped pineapple (about 1 pineapple), if you can't, canned pineapple ones will work, but try to get a fresh pineapple first
- 3 medium oranges peeled and separate in segments
- 1/2 cup orange juice
- 2 Tablespoons lemon juice
- 1 tablespoon lemon zest
- 2 Tablespoons raw honey
- 2 cups soy milk or coconut milk, your preference

Makes: 4-6

Total Prep Time: 60 minutes + before you can eat them!

MMMMMMMMMMMMMMMMMMMMMMMMMMMMM

Preparation:

Prepare the fresh fruits as indicated in the list of ingredients.

Add the pineapple and oranges in the blender, along with the orange juice, lemon juice, lemon zest and raw honey.

Activate until the fruits have blended nicely.

Add the milk and do it again.

Pour the final mixture into the popsicle molds and freeze for several hours.

Enjoy these delicious treats later.

(25) Berries Popsicles in A Bowl

I am not literal when I say we are making popsicles in a bowl. We are making popsicles in molds, but then serving them in a bowl. The reason why is simple, it is because they are being served with fresh berries, a perfect addition.

List of Ingredients:

- 1 cup fresh raspberries
- 1 cup fresh blueberries
- 1 cup cherry juice
- 3 Tablespoons white sugar
- 2 cups 2% milk
- 2 Tablespoons lemon juice
- Whipped cream
- Chopped peanuts

Makes: 4-6

Total Prep Time: 60 minutes + before you can eat them!

MMMMMMMMMMMMMMMMMMMMMMMMMMMMM

Preparation:

Use half of the fresh fruits in the popsicles mixture, save the other half in the refrigerator for now.

Add the fruits in the blender with the sugar, milk, lemon juice and cherry juice.

Blend until the mixture is nice and smooth.

Pour into small popsicle molds.

Freeze for a few hours before you can unmold them.

Use some dessert bowls, and unmold the popsicles upside down, serve with whipped cream, fresh whole fruits and nuts.

About the Author

A native of Indianapolis, Indiana, Valeria Ray found her passion for cooking while she was studying English Literature at Oakland City University. She decided to try a cooking course with her friends and the experience changed her forever. She enrolled at the Art Institute of Indiana which offered extensive courses in the culinary Arts. Once Ray dipped her toe in the cooking world, she never looked back.

When Valeria graduated, she worked in French restaurants in the Indianapolis area until she became the head chef at one of the 5-star establishments in the area. Valeria's attention to taste and visual detail caught the eye of a local business person who expressed an interest in publishing her recipes. Valeria began her secondary career authoring cookbooks and e-books which she tackled with as much talent and gusto as her first career. Her passion for food leaps off the page of her books which have colourful anecdotes and stunning pictures of dishes she has prepared herself.

Valeria Ray lives in Indianapolis with her husband of 15 years, Tom, her daughter, Isobel and their loveable Golden Retriever, Goldy. Valeria enjoys cooking special dishes in her large, comfortable kitchen where the family gets involved in preparing meals. This successful, dynamic chef is an inspiration to culinary students and novice cooks everywhere.

••••••••• ● ● ● ● ● ● ● ●•••••

Author's Afterthoughts

Thank you for Purchasing my book and taking the time to read it from front to back. I am always grateful when a reader chooses my work and I hope you enjoyed it!

With the vast selection available online, I am touched that you chose to be purchasing my work and take valuable time out of your life to read it. My hope is that you feel you made the right decision.

I very much would like to know what you thought of the book. Please take the time to write an honest and informative review on Amazon.com. Your experience and opinions will be of great benefit to me and those readers looking to make an informed choice.

With much thanks,

Valeria Ray

Made in the USA
Coppell, TX
06 June 2021